The Everyday Enlightenment Journal

The Everyday Enlightenment Journal

Dan Millman

ONE SPIRIT

One Spirit, 1271 Avenue of the Americas, New York, NY 10020

Text design by Stanley S. Drate/Folio Graphics Co. Inc.

Printed in the United States of America

Introduction

Hidden within the changing fortunes of our everyday lives is a deep yearning for understanding and for peace. In the quiet hours, in rare moments of repose and openness, our souls seek the sacred truths and intuitive wisdom at the heart of our existence. In such moments of reflection, life's key questions peek like shy children around the corners of our minds: Who am I? we ask. But then a list of daily tasks demands our attention. We wonder, What do I really want? Then the sound of a baby's cry or a loved one's voice takes precedence. We inquire, What is my calling, my larger purpose? Then the phone rings, and we talk of current events before turning our attention to paying the bills. Chores and projects keep coming down the shoot, stacking like dirty dishes and clothing in the hamper. We get so busy with the details, deadlines, programmed plans and immediate goals like putting food on the table, being a good husband, wife, parent, that we may set life's larger questions and even forget to spend quite time alone to explore our deepest yearnings. We do need to attend to life's everyday duties—our work and our families. But let us also attend to our souls. And let us heed the words of Henry David Thoreau, "I went to the woods because I wished to live deliberately; to front only the essential facts of life, and see if I could learn what it had to teach, and not, when I came to die, discover that I had not lived."

Once or twice in a lifetime, something happens to interrupt business as usual—an illness or injury, a financial dislocation, divorce, or death in the family shakes us, and the little things that seemed so important become small stuff. Our perspective expands. We begin to ask again whether there might be a game infinitely larger and more mysterious going on in the very midst of our busy lives. This perspective shift can be disorienting. We may become ungrounded and even a little unglued for a time. But from that confusion flow the bigger questions and larger spiritual truths we had set aside.

Where are we to find the answers? We can't always rely on scientific studies, because studies often come to different conclusions, depending upon who paid for the research. Nor can we count on folk wisdom or wise aphorisms, because they also contradict one another: You can't teach an old dog new tricks—but you're never to old to learn. Opposites attract—but birds of a feather flock together. Absence makes the heart grow fonder—but out of sight, out of mind.

Neither statistical studies nor folk wisdom can lay exclusive claim to truth. We are left with the question, Shall we trust science or mysticism, the masculine or feminine, traditional or alternative medicine, centralized or local government? We are learning at in the end, we need to trust ourselves—our instinct and intuition as well as intellect. Our journey truly begins with the realization that the only certain way to change the world is to begin by changing ourselves. In the words of Friedrich Nietzsche: "If each of us sweeps in front of our own doorstep, the whole world will be clean."

The Magic of Transformation

Magic is the power to change. The magician transforms a bouquet into a turtle dove; the alchemist changes lead into gold-symbols of the internal alchemy of personal evolution as we change from flesh to spirit, from form to formless, from fear to love, from darkness to enlightenment.

Because change is as unpredictable as it is inevitable—and because we fear the unknown—we both desire and resist it. In *Way of the Peaceful Warrior,* during my college years, I assured my old mentor, Socrates, that I was "more than willing to change." He laughed and said, "You're willing to change, all right, Junior—you change your major, your clothing, hairstyle, girlfriends, or residence. It seems to me that you're willing to change nearly anything but yourself." And he was right.

Even if our goal is not so much to change, but to accept ourselves as we are, reaching this goal still involves spiritual growth and change. We are each and all transformed by the winds and tides of change; our only choice is to resist the currents or to ride them. Seneca said that "the fates lead those who will, and drag those who won't." An ancient Chinese proverb reminds us that only the supremely wise-and the ignorant-do no change.

During my years as an athlete and university coach, I constantly searched for the secrets of positive change. I discovered that talent for sport could be developed—that athletic success came from a solid foundation of strength, suppleness, stamina, and sensitivity, then a step-by-step learning process.

After I won a world championship, and later, coached the top U.S. Olympian in gymnastics, I began to think that maybe I was onto something.

But I also learned rather quickly that athletic prowess wasn't much help when I went out on a date, or got married, or had children. My interests and inquiries began to extend beyond the gymnasium and into the arena of everyday life, where I explored what qualities could be developed to generate a talent for living— qualities that would help to generate success in every facet of daily life. This inquiry led me into the realms of mind and heart, to the twelve gateways—twelve catalysts of personal growth that lead to a happier, more meaningful and abundant life. The athletic realm had taught me well that knowing is only a beginning, a map. Then comes the doing, the journey.

That is why this companion volume to *Everyday Enlightenment* is, above all, a call to action, a chance to reinvent your life, reawaken the light within you, and refresh your spirit. If *Everyday Enlightenment* is your map for the journey, here is your personal journal to record your own insights and aspirations. Herein you can reflect upon the transformative principles, practices, and perspectives as they apply to your life, to make them your own. So use it, mark in it, write down your thoughts, ideas, and dreams on its pages. In the same way you might personalize a new home, make this book a spiritual home by filling it with your personal insights and aspirations.

As a human being, you now stand between heaven and earth,

with your head in the clouds and your feet on the ground. You represent spiritual potential in the material world. But potential is only potential until you act. The quality of your life depends upon how well you turn what you know into what you do. This power of doing is the alchemical secret of manifestation—transforming mind into matter. It can begin with the written word.

A proverb says, "I hear and I forget; I see and I remember; I do and I understand." Writing is the beginning of doing, a way of bringing the abstract into reality. How many times have we had feelings or thoughts we couldn't quite clarify until we had to say or write them? Physically writing down your goals, your dreams and aspirations, is a first step in manifesting them. This journal builds a bridge between knowing and doing, between wishing and becoming.

What if Thomas Edison, Amelia Earhart, Michelangelo Buonarroti, Marie Curie, Ludwig von Beethoven, Leonardo da Vinci, Joan of Arc, Auguste Renoir, and Martin Luther King, Jr.—inventors, artists, musicians, and spiritual leaders throughout history—had failed to act upon their visions? What if Columbus had turned around when the seas got stormy and gone home? No one would have blamed him. Or remembered him, either. Vince Havner reminds us, "It's not enough to stare up the steps unless you also step up the stairs." The Tagore of India wrote, "You cannot cross the sea merely by staring at the water." The smallest good deed is more powerful than the grandest good intention. Turning intention into action can change your life. In fact, it is the only way to change your life.

We have more control over our behaviors then over our thoughts or feelings. So begin by changing what you say and do. Begin here. Begin now. Begin in small ways, with little things. Simple is powerful. A little bit of something is better than a lot of nothing. Tiny gestures are the seeds from which grow your life-style, character, and self-respect. Your mind determines what you want; your actions determine what you receive. You don't have to travel far—just take the next step.

There are only two things you have to do in life: You have to die; and you have to live until you die. The rest is up to you. You get to make it up as you go along. Self-worth comes from doing what is worthy. Each day has 24 hours; how you use your time, how you spend your spare moments, is how you spend your life. Don't wait until you have time. Make the time to make a change. And change your life moment by moment, starting now.

It has been said that there are three kinds of people: Those who make things happen; those who watch things happen; and those who wonder what happened. Taking action is not easy in this world, or in our lives. Forces of doubt and inertia exist even in our minds and our bodies. Action requires energy, sacrifice, and courage. To act is to risk, to overcome insecurity, to hurdle past self-doubt, lethargy, apathy, excuses, alibis, and a hundred good reasons to leave it alone, to not rock the boat. So many of us wait for permission to act—wait for motivation, inspiration, or divine guidance before we will act. Some of us act (or react) only when faced with a crisis—a breakup or divorce, a layoff, or the dislocations of an illness or death in the family. Yet in any moment, in this moment, you can make a transcendental leap by acting in accord with your higher goals whether or not you happen to feel like it. In moments like these, you are truly alive. In moments like these, you remember who you are and what you are made of.

This moment is a moment of truth.

Everyday Enlightenment is yours to read; this journal is yours to write. Such writing is an act of remembrance, of devotion, of passion—a reminder about what is important-what really matters. So write your words, your thoughts, your passions on the page as only you can write it. And as you write, reflect upon each gateway as it manifests in your life.

The Twelve Gateways to Personal Growth

These Gateways lend themselves perfectly to a twelve-week program—covering one gateway each week—reflecting on and applying key principles of that gateway each day.

The first week, explore your self-worth and how it influences your choices and interactions with others. Ask yourself, "How good can I stand it today?" Open up a little (or a lot) more to life's gifts and simple pleasures.

The second week, reclaim the power of will and self-discipline. Notice how you can do what you need to do whether or not you feel like it. And when you engage your will, overtime, your goals will become destinations you know you can reach, one step at a time.

The third week, focus on physical energy and vitality, using this week as a period of physical rejuvenation, experimenting with diet and exercise to experience greater balance, lightness, ease, and well-being.

The fourth week, pay special attention to your relationship to (and issues with) money. Resolve to set into motion—into mind and heart and down on paper in this journal—a clear plan to greater abundance and stability through acts of giving and receiving.

The fifth week, direct your attention into your own mind; spend (more) time meditating, or simply noticing and writing down your thoughts as they arise for a period of time. Notice where attention flows during the day so you can live more fully-with greater clarity and awareness.

The sixth week, whenever appropriate, place special emphasis on trusting your intuitive abilities in making decisions large and small. If you feel that you don't know what to do, assume that you do know; trust your inner guidance system and live in the light of faith in your own inner guidance system, trusting in a higher will working through you.

The seventh week is a time to let your emotional colors flow richly upon the canvas of everyday life. Write down a few words to describe your feelings at fifteen minutes after the hour for a whole day. Notice how emotions come and go like the weather. Embrace them then let them go their way with full acceptance. Free your feelings so they can liberate you.

The eighth week, take psychological and emotional (not necessarily physical) risks. Confront your everyday fears. Dramatic physical challenges such as fire walking or sky diving are less important than overcoming such fears as: sharing a truth, expressing a feeling, speaking in public, asking for help or forgiveness. Say you are sorry. Allow yourself to look silly or foolish in your relationships. Celebrate the courage of everyday life.

The ninth week, even while performing duties at home and work, make more time for silence, solitude, self-reflection, and writing in your journal. Dedicate this week to honest self-examination. Each evening, apply the three-question reality check to a different person so you can come to know yourself more realistically in relationship to others, thereby finding compassion, humility, and gratitude.

The tenth week, consciously celebrate life's sensual pleasures—not just sexuality, but sight, sound, smell, touch, taste. Remember the joy of being alive while you can. Explore your sexual and sensual indulgence and denial, your inhibitions and spontaneity, your puritan and hedonist tendencies. Find balance and joy. Create special treats or occasions. Then enjoy them. Embrace your sexuality. Enjoy yourself. Celebrate your sensuality. Allow yourself the pleasure of being fully alive.

The eleventh week, make a special effort to see others in your world with compassion. Remember that all of us were once tiny infants and each of us will one day lose loved ones, will die. Remember that everyone—the rich and poor, the meek and mighty—have all known pain, doubt, and sorrow. Take the risk. Open your heart to the sorrows of the world so that you may also open to the joys. Write a list of people past or present you have wronged and ask their forgiveness. Express loving-kindness even when you don't feel loving or kind, and your vulnerable heart will find more love in the world.

The twelfth week, find some way each day to provide a service, no matter how small, for friend, loved one, or stranger. This service might come in the form of kind words, an appreciative note, an offer of help or encouragement. Volunteer for a week-end project. Pick up some litter. Make each place you visit and each person you see a little brighter for your having been there. Make yourself useful by making a difference. And in doing so, find a new sense of connection, meaning, and purpose in the world.

Twelve weeks—three months, one season of the year—can begin a new and enlightened lifestyle. Only you hold the keys to the twelve gateways in your life. Practice makes perfect. Practice begins an irreversible learning process that expands your relationship to everyday life in each and every moment. A life that may have seemed mundane, confused, or pointless becomes an adventure course, a spiritual school. Here is a chance to follow your heart's desire—to have, to do, to live the life you were born to live.

As you proceed through the pages of this journal, making them your own with your words and dreams upon the page, notice which of the gateways interest you the least—which seem difficult or boring. For these very gateways will forge the spiritual chain of head and hand and heart. Experience the power of commitment as you put all the pieces of the puzzle in place, and your life becomes a process of personal and spiritual growth. The quotations and excerpts on the pages of this journal are only reminders of what you know but might have forgotten. The words are mine, but not the wisdom, which is as perennial as the trees and stars, and common to us all. Each of us are writers, singers, artists, poets, athletes, sages, and musicians. Our level of expertise will depend upon how far we choose to climb along a particular path.

Ultimately, your journey through the twelve gateways and through this journal reveals to you that enlightenment is not just something you feel—it is something you do, and something you share. Here's wishing you many moments of enlightened action. May your deeds serve others as they enrich your life and fill your world with light.

Dan Millman

THE

FIRST GATEWAY

Discover Your Worth

No matter how intelligent, attractive, or talented you may be—
to the degree you doubt your worthiness
you tend to sabotage your efforts
and undermine your relationships.
Life is full of gifts and opportunities;
you will open to receive and enjoy them
to the degree that you begin to
appreciate your innate worth,
and to offer to yourself
the same compassion and respect
that you would give to others.
Discovering your worth
sets your spirit free.

Life is full of gifts and opportunities;
you need only to open your arms,
your heart, your mind, and your life.

If we can just trust God enough to let go of who we think we have to be before we can be ourselves, we will find that the greatest gift that God has given us is who we already are.

No one else is more qualified than we are to make our decisions and know what is best for us. Love of Self is to know and trust thy Self.

This very moment is the only moment we have. Life is now. We live in an eternal now. When we are awake and present, we are truly alive.

The tasks that have been entrusted to us are often difficult. Almost everything that matters is difficult, and everything matters.

A fire was in my head and in my heart, but most of all, in my soul. I had discovered my soul.

The Divine is everywhere and exists within even the most intimate details of our lives. All that we experience today has its purpose in tomorrow's events; sometimes, the purpose is not evident for years of tomorrows. We cannot, and indeed we must not, even ~~always~~ attempt to believe we know what is best for us. The Divine will reveal its plan for us; we have to be open to receive it.

"Let nothing disturb you. God Alone Suffices. Teresa of Avila."

Even though you don't always feel kind, or brave, or deserving, life continues to offer support in myriad ways.

 No one else can give you an improved sense of self-worth;
You increase sense of worth by doing what is worthy.

"Self-respect is the fruit of self-discipline."
—**Abraham Heschel**

Your innate worth has never been compromised
or touched by fate or circumstance.

You cannot raise your worth;
you can only discover it.

Success results from talent, effort, and creativity,
but requires a willingness to receive.

Key questions: How deserving am I?
How good can I stand it today?

To the degree you value your innate worth,
so will your subconscious mind
open up to accept life's bounty.

"Rain may pour down from the heavens,
but if you only hold up a thimble,
a thimbleful is all you receive."

—Ramakrishna

You subconsciously choose, attract, and experience
according to what you believe you deserve.

How much do you really believe you deserve?
Notice your life right now.

The current state of your relationships, work,
finances, education, and health
reflects and reveals your perceived worth.

Even fame and fortune have a downside
for those who feel undeserving.

The moment you recognize the degree
to which your difficulties are self-imposed,
you begin to heal them.

End self-sabotage and take charge of your life
by taking responsibility for
the choices and actions you make.

Life is an unearned gift.
This is the hidden meaning of grace.

You cannot change past mistakes,
but you can avoid repeating them.

Your worth does not depend on being perfect.

Discovering your worth is a first step
to practicing everyday enlightenment.

As you rediscover your worth,
you discover the worth of all beings.

THE
SECOND GATEWAY

Reclaim Your Will

*Inside you is untapped strength
of will, of spirit, of heart.
The kind of strength that will not flinch
in the face of adversity.
You have only to remember your purpose,
the vision that brought you to Earth—
the vision that will take you to the stars—
to the depths of the oceans and
up the stairway to the soul.
Great strength of will
resides within you,
waiting for expression.*

The greatest human freedom
is the power of free will.

Reclaim your will
and you reclaim your life.

"When running up a hill,
it is all right to give up as many times as you wish,
as long as your feet keep moving."
—Shoma Morita, M.D.

Life's greatest challenge
is turning what you know
into what you do.

The best way to do
what you need or want to do
is to just do it.

Difficulties can stop you only
if you doubt the power of your will.

The will is like a muscle;
it grows stronger with use.

Your inner strength is waiting to be called forth,
to grow stronger still.

There is no better time than now
to remember, rebuild, reawaken, and reclaim
your innate powers of will.

By paying attention to each day, each moment,
you see what needs to be done right now.

Knowing your higher purpose
and acting in alignment with that purpose
unleashes the full force of your will.

No matter what your purpose,
obstacles will appear between you and your goals
to test and strengthen you.

Willpower is like an all-terrain vehicle;
it drives you around the obstacles, past the
stumbling blocks, over hurdles, through
doubt and uncertainty, sending you onward
to your destiny.

Pursue your dreams!
Creation follows vision;
willpower begins with a wish and a prayer.

Stay flexible but resolute;
bend like the willow in a wind
then snap back!

Celebrate each and every time
you apply your will to
accomplish your wishes.

To become an everyday success,
pick small, do-able goals;
then do them.

A little bit of something
is better than a lot of nothing.

When you feel as if you've lost your will
have you actually forgotten your purpose
and lost your way?

Daily life is a form of spiritual weight lifting,
you are here to strengthen your spirit.

By focusing your attention,
you focus your will.

Resistance to change is a fact of life.
Once a pattern is in place,
we all tend to resist change.

You can depend upon your will,
because it comes from within you.

The power of your will is a master key
to everyday enlightenment,
and to all the gateways to come.

THE

THIRD GATEWAY

Energize Your Body

*Your body is the only thing
you are guaranteed to keep for a lifetime.
It forms the foundation of your earthly existence.
Energizing your body
enriches your life
by enhancing every human capacity.
If you lack vitality,
nothing else really matters;
if you have your health,
anything is possible.*

You did not make the body,
but it is in your soul's keeping.
Your body is the only possession
you are guaranteed to keep for a lifetime.

Energizing your body enriches your life
by amplifying every human capacity.

"Your body is the ground and metaphor of your life, the expression of your existence. It is your Bible, your encyclopedia, your life story. Everything that happens to you is stored and reflected in your body. In the marriage of flesh and spirit, divorce is impossible."

—Gabrielle Roth

If you don't take care of your body,
where will you live?

If you lack vitality, nothing else really matters;
if you have your health, anything is possible.

 Take one slow, deep breath,
as slowly and deeply as you can—
inhale light, healing, and vitality;
exhale and let go—
feel a moment of enlightenment.

Energizing your body begins
by making peace with and coming to love
the body you've been given.

No matter where your flights of fancy take
you, you return to a fundamental truth:
The human journey begins and
ends with the body.

How can you be short of energy?
You are made of it!

The cornerstones of an energized life include
moderate, regular exercise;
a simple, healthful diet;
enough fresh air, fresh water, and rest;
and engaging in a creative activity.

"I am convinced that a light supper, a good night's sleep, and a fine morning have sometimes made a hero of the same man who, by an indigestion, a restless night, and rainy morning, would have proved a coward."

—Lord Chesterfield

Do you want to travel out of your body before you've really gotten into it?

It is not enough to know about or appreciate the trinity of good health—diet, exercise and rest; to reap their benefits, you need to make them absolute priorities.

Make a healthy lifestyle more important than career, or money, or television programs, and you will find greater joy in your career, finances, and recreation.

"Never eat more than you can lift."
—**Miss Piggy**

One of the best ways of increasing the quality and quantity of life is through en-lightened diet.

You can live for weeks without food and days without water, but only minutes without breathing. Oxygen is free. Indulge yourself.

One of the primary goals of spiritual awareness is to make conscious habits that were previously unconscious, thereby transforming them.

Walking is the most natural everyday exercise
with myriad benefits.

As you greet neighbors, view the changing
textures of light and shadow,
you transform a walk into a spiritual experience.

If breathing is a key to longevity,
relaxation is a key to energy.

Breathe deeply, and relax as much as you can
in everything you do.

Relaxation is perhaps the most important
life-skill you can ever learn.

As you consciously relax,
even in difficult moments,
your body returns to a natural state of ease,
of everyday enlightenment.

THE
FOURTH GATEWAY

Manage Your Money

Money is neither god nor devil,
but a form of energy.
Like love or fear,
it can serve you or bind you,
depending upon how you manage it.
By clarifying your goals
and using your gifts,
you can make good money,
doing what you enjoy,
while serving
the highest calling of your soul.
Using money wisely, and well,
you increase the material
and spiritual wealth
with your world.

Money is neither god nor devil;
it is merely a form of energy.

Spend your energy wisely, and well.

"There's a certain Buddhistic calm
that comes from having money in the bank."
—**Tom Robbins**

Using your own money wisely in giving and
receiving, you share your material and
spiritual wealth with the world.

Clarify your goals and use your gifts
to make good money, doing what you enjoy,
while serving other people.

In the context of personal and spiritual growth,
money is more than a means of exchange or ready cash.
Money represents survival, security, safety, shelter,
food, family, livelihood.

Your relationship to money leads to self-knowledge—it reflects your relationship to service and spirit, calls you to function boldly in society, and challenges you to discover your worth.

Notice what money teaches about your ability to receive and to give.

Managing your money is a spiritual discipline
because it frees your attention and awareness
to notice the beauty of life.

Simple principles of sufficiency:
Live below your means.
Pay yourself first.
Create a budget and stick to it.

"Money, it turned out, was a lot like sex.
You thought of nothing else if you didn't have it
and thought of other things when you did."

—James Baldwin

What you believe about money
will influence your ability to acquire it.

"I don't like money, actually, but it quiets my nerves."

—**Joe Louis**

Managing your money well doesn't require magic or miracles— only an honest examination of your values, beliefs, and behaviors.

"It is better to have a permanent income
than to be fascinating."

—Oscar Wilde

As with any form of energy, money needs to move,
to be channeled wisely and well.

"Money doesn't have any soul, but we do,
and we're the people through whom money flows
and with which money speaks."

—Lynne Twist

As you share your material abundance,
spiritual wealth pours down from the heavens,
bathing you in its light.

Right livelihood means finding work that matches
your values and interest
while challenging your capacities.

Finding the inherent meaning in whatever you do
is one of life's greatest blessings.

The secret of satisfying work
is to provide quality, even artfulness, in whatever you do.

Your work becomes a path of personal and spiritual growth

as you use it to serve, connect, to make your labor
an offering for the good of the larger community.

"He is well paid that is well satisfied."
—**William Shakespeare**

As your actions begin to flow from an
expanded sense of worth, you begin to
accept, attract, and receive more from the
world— not just money, but friendship,
love, and attention.

THE
FIFTH GATEWAY

Tame Your Mind

*You perceive the world
through an obscure window
of beliefs, interpretations, and associations.
The world is therefore
a reflection of your mind.
As your mind clears,
you perceive reality
simply as it is.
What does your experience of life
reveal about your filters of perception?*

Make peace with your mind.

As you tame your mind
by training your attention,
you simplify your life.

"With our thoughts, we make the world."
—Gautama Buddha

What does your experience of life
reveal about your filters of perception?

You perceive the world through an obscured window filtered and colored by beliefs, interpretations, and associations.

The world is therefore
a reflection of your mind.

Reality is not what you think.

As your mind clears,
you perceive reality as it is.

You clear the doors of perception by noticing
how arising thoughts and beliefs impact
your experience of life.

You do not see reality as it is;
you see the world as you are.
Reality is as you believe it is.

Thoughts are like the stuff of dreams;
they arise from the psyche
like waves on the sea or clouds in the sky.

Thoughts happen.
They are no problem unless we believe them.

In a given moment, your attention resides in one of two worlds: the objective world of what is happening, or the subjective world of your thoughts about what is happening.

Life has no consistent meanings; you project your own meanings onto life.

"The mind in itself,
can make a heaven of hell,
a hell of heaven."
—John Milton

Look up! Notice the beauty and the mystery of life.
Stop thinking and there
is nothing you cannot know.

By accepting events, thoughts and feelings as they are, while making the best of life, you reduce suffering and let life flow.

Acceptance is a practice of everyday enlightenment.

Meditation involves gentle vigilance and commitment to stay aware of what is happening in this moment. It is no more and no less spiritual than paying attention to how you tie your shoes.

Release a thought
as you would release a fish,
back into the stream.

"We are here and it is now.
Further than that
all human knowledge is moonshine."
—H.L. Mencken

There is no need to fix or quiet
or do anything about your mind.
Just let it be.
This is the highest meditation.

Only now exists.
Past and future are illusions in the mind.

You only have this moment.

THE

SIXTH GATEWAY

Trust
Your Intuition

*Below everyday awareness
is a shamanlike, childlike consciousness—
weaver of dreams, keeper of instinct.
Your subconscious holds keys to
a treasure house of intuitive wisdom,
clear sight, and untapped power.
All you have to do is to
look, listen, and trust,
paying attention to
dreams, feelings, instinct.
If you can't trust your own inner senses,
what can you trust?*

Below everyday awareness is a shamanlike,
childlike consciousness
—weaver of dreams, keeper of instinct.

Few of us fully trust our inner guidance system.
We can trust what we know
only when we know what we have.

"There is no need to run outside for better
seeing—rather, abide at the
center of your being"

—Lao-tzu

Trusting your intuition
is trusting God or Spirit;
speaking to you and through you.

You have only to look, listen, and trust,
paying attention to dreams, feelings, instinct.

The subconscious holds keys to a treasure
house of intuitive wisdom, clear sight, and
untapped power.

"The decisions of human life usually have far more to do with the instincts . . . than with conscious will and well-meaning reasonableness."

—Carl Jung

Everyday enlightenment means using both sides of your brain, integrating logic and intuition, conscious and subconscious, science and mysticism, to form a full representation of reality.

When you understand the natural
rather than the magical nature of intuition,
you begin to trust your innate ability to know
without knowing how you know.

Intuitive decisions are based upon
your subconscious mission and destiny
of which your reasoning mind is
most often unaware.

To access and trust your intuitive powers,
stop being so reasonable!
Trust the mind, but listen well to the heart's quiet voice.

Trusting intuition may involve following odd impressions
without consciously understanding why.
Doing so, you may meet opportunities
that might otherwise have escaped you.

We all have access to a vast and mysterious
storehouse of intuitive wisdom.

By listening respectfully to your subconscious
stirrings, you reconnect to the simple
truths at the heart of life.

Prayer may be the highest,
most personal and powerful way
to access intuitive guidance.

Other people's perspectives can be helpful at
times, but the sixth gateway is about trusting
your own inner guidance. Intuition is a
do-it-yourself project.

You are an oracle: You are the expert
on your own life and destiny;
no one knows you
better than you can know yourself.

The world is an oracle;
you can find guidance in any moment of openness,
while watching a tree bending in the wind;
you can make meaning out of the shapes of clouds;
the changing seasons or a winding stream winding
can lend life-changing insights.

Stop. Look. Listen. And there is nothing you
cannot know. Trust is the key that
opens the sixth gateway.

 "When you come to a fork in the road, take it."
—**Yogi Berra**

There are two sides to every issue—and every brain: The left brain has analysis and reason, but without the right brain's intuitive guidance, decisions come out half-baked.

Balance and blend the right and left, inside and out, East and West, logic and intuition.

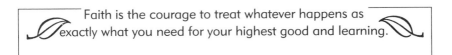
Faith is the courage to treat whatever happens as exactly what you need for your highest good and learning.

Transcendental truth informs you
that you cannot make a wrong decision,
Life won't always give you what you want,
but it will consistently give you what you need.

THE

SEVENTH GATEWAY

Accept Your Emotions

*Emotions are like waves on the sea
or weather in the skies,
rising and passing of their own accord.
You cannot control your feelings
by an act of intention or will.
So you are not responsible for your feelings;
only for your response to them.
Accept emotions completely,
let your feelings be;
just don't let them run your life.*

Emotions come and go like waves on the sea,
rising and falling of their own accord.

You are not responsible for what you cannot control;
and you cannot control your feelings—
only your response to them.

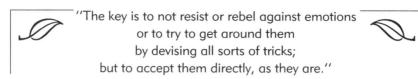

"The key is to not resist or rebel against emotions
or to try to get around them
by devising all sorts of tricks;
but to accept them directly, as they are."

—Takahisa Kora, M.D.

Accept your emotions completely,
but don't let them run your life.

If life is a journey, then emotions
are the weather fronts you pass through,
and that pass through you, along the way.

Accepting your emotions (and the emotions of others)
serves to heal and rejuvenate all your relationships,
from acquaintances to intimates.

You don't have to change your feelings;
just change your relationship to them.

 Welcoming all emotions, you begin to feel life
in living color rather than black and white.

To accept your emotions,
you have to know them.

Of the two levels of emotional
authenticity—knowing your feelings and
expressing them—knowing is the
most important.

Expressing your feelings can show courage and honesty and provide useful feedback to others on the impact of their words or deeds.

Expressing your truth in a respectful way makes it more likely to be heard.

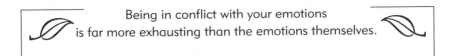

Being in conflict with your emotions
is far more exhausting than the emotions themselves.

Weather of not you lifke arising feelings,
accept them as you would accept
drizzles or snow flurries.

Accepting your emotions may mean appreciating the positive lessons contained even in negative emotions.

If you are to accept your own emotions, you need to accept others' emotions as well.

Balance your breathing.

Breathing evenly and deeply into your belly
won't necessarily make the feelings go away,
but you will rebalance your body and psyche
so that you can speak or act more effectively.

Attend to your posture.

Body, mind, and emotions interpenetrate one another.
Just as emotions influence your posture,
so posture influences emotions.

Remember to relax.

When you relax, it is very difficult
to feel angry or afraid.

Life is a series of moments.
No one feels the same way all the time.

As you mature in the seventh gateway, the time will come
when you transcend your emotions—
not because they have gone away,
but because you have made peace with them.

THE

EIGHTH GATEWAY

Face Your Fears

Fear is a wonderful servant,
but a terrible master.
Like pain, it can alert and advise you,
but may also cloud or limit your life.
Fear appears in many disguises, such as
"I'm not really interested in doing that"
or "Why bother?" or "I can't."
You face fear every day—
fear of failure, of rejection,
even the fear of being yourself.
Your fears are not walls, but hurdles.
Courage is not the absence of fear,
but the conquering of it.

Fear is a wonderful servant, but a terrible master.

 Fear appears in many disguises, such as,
"I'm not really interested in doing that" or
"Why bother?" or "I can't."

"Avoiding danger is no safer
in the long run than outright exposure.
The fearful are caught as often as the bold."
—Helen Keller

Fears are not walls, but hurdles.

You don't have to control the fear;
just don't let it control you.

Fear, like any adversary;
can also serve as your guide and advisor.

However or wherever you hide from our fears,
you will eventually face them.

When you face what you fear,
you will be filled with energy and light.

Whether fear is your friend or foe
depends upon whether you become
its master or its servant.

Take a stand; step forward resolutely
into the life you were born to live.

The primary way to face your fear
is by taking action.

Courage is not the absence of fear,
but the conquering of it;
the more fear you feel,
the more courage you show by acting.

This the ancient warriors knew:
To vanquish the enemy, you must understand it.

The deeper your understanding, the greater your power.
Awareness dissolves fear at its core.

Sometimes you have to make a leap of faith
and grow your wings on the way down.

 One act of everyday courage calls forth others—
little decisions and acts that shape your life
and inspire others to do the same.

Expectations tend to shape your perception of life;
fearful expectations create a fear-filled life.

Begin to visualize positive outcomes—
form the pictures you desire rather
than the images you fear.

Fear is a wall to scale, a hurdle to leap,
a challenge to meet, a call to action.

You cannot control your fear,
but you can slow your breathing,
shake your arms loose, and relax your muscles.

"Many of our fears are tissue-paper thin,
and a single courageous step
would carry us clear through them."
—**Brendan Francis**

Those of us with the strongest fears
gain the most from facing them.

Fears diminish as skills improve.
Competence breeds confidence.

There are few more joyous words in life than, "I did it!"
Each time you face your fears,
you practice everyday enlightenment.

THE

NINTH GATEWAY

Illuminate Your Shadow

As an infant, you were pure potential,
full and whole, open and authentic,
yielding and powerful, good and bad,
disciplined and spontaneous,
a container of possibilities.
In growing up,
you disowned parts of your being
that conflicted with emerging values.
Creating false self-images,
you became "this" but not "that."
Hidden opposites will have their day;
it's what you don't see that can hurt you.
By illuminating your shadow,
you become whole again, and real.
Releasing energy once bound
in defense of self-image,
you find energy, understanding,
humility, and compassion.

By illuminating your shadow side
with the light of awareness,
you again become whole and real.

As an infant, you were yielding and powerful,
good and bad, a container of possibilities—
you were authentic and whole.

"Everyone is a moon
and has a dark side
which he never shows to anybody."
—Mark Twain

Your shadow is what you insist you are not,
the dust you sweep under
the rug of your awareness.

Everything contains its opposite.
You contain all things high and low;
within you are saint and sinner, moralist and libertine.

Sometimes you have to deal with the darkness
before you can see the light.

"The life which is unexamined
is not worth living."

—Plato

The shadow realm is the abode of fallen angels
and phantom fears,
where illusions die,
giving birth to truth and reality.

"There is no light without shadow
and no psychic wholeness without imperfection."
—Carl Jung

Illuminating your shadow
is not about inviting the devil to dinner or
allowing your negative qualities or impulses
to influence your behavior.

It's what you don't see
that can hurt you.

When you have seen your dark side,
you can make a more conscious choice
about how you will be and do in the world.

"No one can become conscious of the
shadow without . . . recognizing the
dark aspects of the personality
as present and real."

—Carl Jung

Explore your dark forest not by chopping
through it with a sword of blame but by
illuminating it with a beacon of compassion.
Welcome your shadow into the
house of your spirit.

You cannot accept yourself until
you know yourself.

Only when you know and accept yourself as
you are, can you understand and accept
others in your world.

By illuminating your shadow
you also reclaim your light.

Releasing energy previously bound up
in defending self-imagery,
you find new vitality, humility, and compassion.

When you illuminate these parts,
you can channel their expression
in positive and constructive ways.

When you write in a journal,
paint on a canvas, or act on a stage,
you shed light on the shadow,
and bring your shadow to the light.

Illuminating your shadow reveals that
Spirit continually supports and blesses you
whether or not you happen to feel deserving.

The blessings of Spirit shower upon you
in a hundred forms every day.

THE

TENTH GATEWAY

Embrace Your Sexuality

*Hungers and appetites
—for sexual release, for food, for life—
are as natural to you
as clouds are to the sky or waves to the sea.
If you suppress or exploit
the surging power of your drives,
you create obsessions, compulsions,
and guilty secrets.
Life is not a matter of
indulging or denying
the energies of life,
but observing, accepting,
and wisely channeling them.
Embracing your sexuality
celebrates your humanity.*

Embracing your sexuality
celebrates your humanity.

Sexuality is your fundamental relationship to
pleasure, your connection to creativity's
fountain of rising energies, your passionate
intercourse with life, your communion with
Spirit through the arms of your lover.

"Lord, give me chastity and self-restraint,
but do not give it yet."

—St. Augustine

Life is not a matter of indulging or denying
the energies of life, but observing, accepting,
and wisely channeling them.

Enlightened sexuality has less to do with
your skills of foreplay
than your capacity for
intimacy and pleasure in every aspect of life.

Embracing your sexuality is not about having
more sex or less; it is about an enlightened
expression of sexual intimacy in the context of
personal and spiritual growth.

Sexuality, a primal directive and drive,
can lead you to communion with God
through ego-transcending union with our partner.

Express who you are!
Know that you are worthy of love.

Never be afraid to ask why.
Never be afraid to ask why not.

Whatever faith we practice,
we need to realize that sexuality
has no more inherent morality or immorality
than eating food or drinking water.

"I'm just a person trapped inside
a woman's body."

—Elaine Boosler

In finding a balance between self-indulgence and self-denial,
you come closer to embracing your sexuality
resolutely, lovingly, and responsibly.

Bring your sexual shadows into the light of
awareness, and in a spirit of compassion,
accept who you are.

The answer to the perceived dilemmas of sexuality
is not a choice between flesh and spirit,
but the healing embrace and integration of both.

"Puritanism—the haunting fear that
someone, somewhere, may be happy."
—H.L. Mencken

Awareness of both your puritanical and
hedonistic tendencies helps you to balance
and reconcile them.

Your sexual evolution involves connecting
your body and physical senses to your
emotional and spiritual core.

The answer to the perceived dilemmas of sexuality
is not a choice between flesh and spirit,
but the healing embrace and integration of both.

Embracing your sexuality sometimes means
losing your mind and coming to your senses.

 Sexual intimacy takes many forms
and represents many states of awareness,
from lust to reassurance to service to communion.

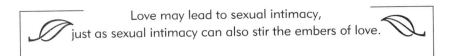
Love may lead to sexual intimacy,
just as sexual intimacy can also stir the embers of love.

Make love not only with the intent
of getting your share of pleasure,
but as a form of healing you provide your partner.

Soul mates are not found;
they are made.

Honor your sexuality and
travel with a lightened heart,
trusting that your thoughts and fantasies
are part of what makes you unique.

THE

ELEVENTH GATEWAY

Awaken Your Heart

*Love is life's great secret.
It transcends fear and isolation,
guiding you beyond the shallows of sentiment,
to the shores of boundless being.
Love endures not from words or feelings alone,
but from actions that carry you
beyond the interests of separate self,
beyond reason or motive,
to embrace all people, things, and circumstances.
Loving-kindness begins in little ways,
in moments of insight and humility,
in your soul's longing for love's communion,
which waits just on the other side
of your heart's doorway.
You are not here to contact your higher self;
you are here to become it.*

Love is life's greatest secret, its hidden treasure.

As your heart awakens,
you fulfill the promise of your human potential.
The heart is the gateway to all mystical secrets.

"Even the Bible is a closed book
unless we approach it with an open heart."

-—Bill Moyers

Loving-kindness begins in little ways,
in moments of insight,
in your soul's longing for love's communion.

You are not here to contact your higher self;
you are here to become it.

The highest wisdom of the ages
tells us to love, serve, and remember God
in, as, and through everyone and everything.

"We're not falling at all, we are rising in love."
—David Roth

Until hearts awaken,
love remains a word, a puzzle, a desirable goal
rather than a living reality.

Love unconditionally with all your heart—
this is all you ever need to learn, to do, to become
—in this gateway, in this book, in this life.

It takes courage to love in this world,
for all that we love, we one day lose.

The path to love is strewn
not only with rose petals, but with thorns.

You will seek love in safety
until you discover there is no safety in love.

There can be no spirituality
without loving kindness.

Put your attention in your heart.
Feel it. Look at the world with eyes of wonder and love.
Touch from your heart.
Listen from your heart.

When you love, you feel happy;
when you feel happy, you act loving.

To awaken the heart
is to be unreasonably happy.

The more you are able to perceive, love, and
accept the face of Spirit gazing at you
from the mirror, the more you will be
able to love Spirit within others.

If we are each and all the same awareness
shining through a billion separate forms,
then holy love begins with self-love,
for how can you love the world
if you cannot love yourself?

Love the greatest
and most difficult spiritual discipline of all.

Love becomes an action;
happiness is a behavior.
Everyday enlightenment is, above all things,
a loving embrace of the moment.

"Love and do what you will."
—St. Augustine

The heart is God's calling card.
It beats the rhythms of the mystery
of life, hope, inspiration, and love.

THE

TWELFTH GATEWAY

Serve
Your World

*Service is an attitude
founded on the recognition
that the world has supported you,
fed you, taught you, tested you,
whether or not you earned it.
Understanding this simple truth
can move you to do what you can
to repay a boundless debt of gratitude.
Service is both a means and an end,
for in giving to others,
you open yourself
to love, abundance, and inner peace.
You cannot serve others without uplifting yourself.*

Serving others makes heroes and saints of us all.
Serving your world is enlightenment in action.

 When you serve others, you
not only contact your higher self;
you become it.

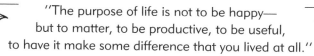

"The purpose of life is not to be happy—
but to matter, to be productive, to be useful,
to have it make some difference that you lived at all."

—Leo Rosten

You cannot serve others without uplifting yourself.

Service is an attitude founded on the recognition
that the world has supported you,
fed you, taught you, and tested you
whether or not you earned it.

Understanding this simple truth
can move you to do what you can
to repay a boundless debt of gratitude.

Name your greatest accomplishment in the world;
now make a list of twenty people
who helped you accomplish it.

Service is both a means and an end,
for in giving to others, you open yourself to love,
abundance, meaning, and connection.

As your own light shines more brightly,
you illuminate the world.

There is no surer or greater path
to embodying the courage and love of your higher self
than self-sacrificing service—
especially when you don't happen to feel like it.

As you transcend limitations and tendencies,
you naturally show loving kindness to others.

Serving those around you—
those you love and those you do not,
in the best way you know how,
is everyday enlightenment.

Ask yourself, and never stop asking,
"How can I begin to share my energy,
my heart, my talent with others?"

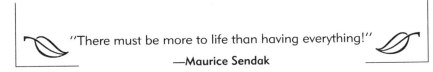
"There must be more to life than having everything!"
—**Maurice Sendak**

Ask yourself, "What would I chose to do
with my time, my life,
if I were already whole and complete?"

Now do it.

"What you are is God's gift to you;
what you make of it is your gift to God."

—Anthony Dalla Villa

Once you awaken to the reality
that you are responsible for your own life,
you come to realize that you are, in a larger sense,
responsible for the entire human family.

"The purpose of life is a life of purpose."
—**Robert Byrne**

Counting our blessings
leads to a desire to give something back.
Thus begins the path of service,
the fruit of our journey,
the gateway to illumination.

"If you have much, give of your wealth;
if you have little, give of your heart."
—**Proverb**

You don't have to be a millionaire
to make a difference;
just ask, "How can I help?"

Remember that small acts can
make a big difference.

As you discover the joy of service,
you may or may not experience dramatic shifts,
or sudden monetary abundance,
but you won't care about that;
you'll be too busy making a positive
difference in this world.

Afterword

In the spiritual traditions there exists a sacred trinity that forms the foundation of personal and spiritual growth. That trinity is comprised of the buddha (teacher), the dharma (teaching), and the sangha (community). It is the third element I address here, because without community, even the finest teacher or most illumined teaching may become like seeds on barren soil. Within the substance and spirit of community, however, our studies and practices are nourished and blossom.

Despite the stories we may hear about wise hermits and sages, spirituality only comes alive within a community of equals, wherein we treat one another as fellow teachers and students; wherein we can test and question one another, mirror one another's strengths and weaknesses, and treat each other as both masters and as fools, with compassion, honesty, and humor. Such a sense of community is a jewel of infinite value.

I presume that you have by now made the journey through the twelve gateways of *Everyday Enlightenment*. I trust that you have actively engaged, considered, reflected upon, and applied these gateways through this experiential journal. If that is the case, then now is the time to join with others; let one become two, and two become three or more, so that together, in moments, you may all become One in the spirit of community.

A great secret of life is that we become our environment. So find a good environment, good company, a circle of friends. Your sense of community is the soil that nourishes your evolution. A supportive group can sustain a new way of life.

Some seekers live within a structured ashram or intentional

community. Despite all the problems and challenges of living within such cloistered places, many are drawn to do so because of our universal need for companionship and intimacy based upon shared values. Those of us who live within our own family households, in everyday neighborhoods, in cities or suburbs, can create a community of three or more like–minded souls who share a common commitment to spiritual growth, to the bigger picture and possibilities of life, to a love of those books, principles, and practices that uplift, clarify, inspire, and heal. Equally important is to include those who have different beliefs and points of view— who will serve as reality checks, who will test us, debate with us, question us, and offer different interpretations. Because if we agree on everything, only one of us is necessary.

In some religious traditions, within the congregation, the minyan, it is recognized that worship is done best within community. Solitude has its value at times, but those who prefer exclusive solitude may become lost or deluded in their isolation, mistaking their opinion for ultimate truth.

No one is smarter than all of us. Group energy can accomplish within a relatively short time what no individual can do alone. Look at the Amish and Mennonites who build a barn in a single day. Observe an automobile or a skyscraper. No one person could have accomplished such wonders; it took thousands. The power of humanity is the power of our differences, the patchwork quilt of varying viewpoints and perspectives finding common ground leading to uncommon love and understanding.

I have received many letters over the years from people yearning for this sense of community, asking, "Where can I meet other people who share my quest?" I can only recommend that you reach out. Use the resources at hand. Seek and you shall find. Visit bookstores, attend seminars, search the internet. Go where others gather in your church, temple, museum, or recital. And above all, remember that even when you sit alone in our room, you are not alone—a million other souls sit with you, and countless angels cheer you on your way.

Before we become spiritual we need to become fully human. If you wish your insights to take root in the world—if you wish to learn and to share your own experience—find or create a support group of two, or three or more people. And interact freely, openly, honestly. Build a foundation of trust by revealing your light and shadow. Become transparent. Come awake within the sacred circle of community. Come alive to both your foolishness and your divinity. Let the layers of armor fall away. Lose yourself and find yourself within a circle of friends. In that circle, minds awaken. Healings happen. Hearts open. And compassion expands beyond the group and into the world.

I close with these reminders: Everyday enlightenment is an ongoing practice. Trying to tie up all the loose ends of life is like trying to eat once and for all. The highest practice is abiding relationship to each arising moment, each surprise, joy, pain, or pleasure. Just say yes. To yourself. To the world. It's all you've got. The twelve gateways are not separate from everyday life. Life's challenges are your schooling, your means of transformation.

And even on the darkest days, never forget that the light of Spirit is there, above the clouds, shining upon you, shining down on us all.

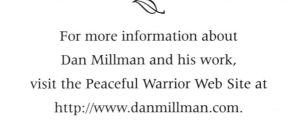

For more information about
Dan Millman and his work,
visit the Peaceful Warrior Web Site at
http://www.danmillman.com.